THE CHARACTER ACTOR CONVENTION

GUY ELSTON

pq

Cover and book design by Jeremy Luke Hill
Cover image by Ellie Hastings
Proofread by Mary Hamilton
Set in Linux Libertine and Slenco
Printed on Coach House Laid
Printed and bound by Arkay Design & Print

LIBRARY AND ARCHIVES CANADA CATALOGUING IN PUBLICATION

Title: The character actor convention / Guy Elston.
Names: Elston, Guy, author.
Identifiers: Canadiana (print) 20250219816 | Canadiana (ebook) 20250225603 |
ISBN 9781774221730 (softcover) | ISBN 9781774221747 (PDF) |
ISBN 9781774221754 (EPUB)
Subjects: LCGFT: Poetry.
Classification: LCC PS8609.L78 C43 2025 | DDC C811/.6—dc23

The Porcupine's Quill gratefully acknowledges the support of the Canada Council for the Arts, the Ontario Arts Council, and the Ontario Book Publishing Tax Credit.

The Porcupine's Quill respectfully acknowledges the ancestral homelands of the Attawandaron, Anishinaabe, Haudenosaunee, and Métis Peoples, and recognizes that we are situated on Treaty 3 territory, the traditional territory of Mississaugas of the Credit First Nation.

The Porcupine's Quill also recognizes and supports the diverse persons who make up its community, regardless of race, age, culture, ability, ethnicity, nationality, gender identity and expression, sexual orientation, marital status, religious affiliation, and socioeconomic status.

The Porcupine's Quill
130 Dublin Street North
Guelph, Ontario, Canada
N1H 4N4
www.porcupinesquill.ca

Contents

I

II

III

IV

Don't clap too loudly—
it's a very old world.

I

The Stake

The night before,
and Joan is certain. As ever.

Do I want to make her wonder?
Or not? *War*

is not as divine as I first thought,

Joan admits. Our game of chess

lies unfinished. The bet:
loser says the one thing they never could.

How can these cassocked frauds judge me,
Joan sighs. *Are you like them?*

I watch a spider sit still.
I don't know. I won't exist much longer.

Aren't you scared?
I ask, fiddling with my fallen bishop.

Oh, I'll burn, Joan laughs.
I do every time. Your move.

Produce (noun)

Minnesota man's 2,749lb pumpkin sets world record

Dear Father,

I've prepared my defence.
4 Your love has made me ridiculous.
Small fortunes spent
on my ballooning—to what end?
Family tradition? I never asked
for a certificate.

Spring temps swing wildly,
frost on fresh buds, secondary vines
clipped to focus energy,
cut tips buried. Good habits win prizes,
not friends—not that you'd know.
Man of science, perfectionist, upscaler.

What if I were tiny but delicious,
what if I burned internally
through carved teeth? Not
an extension of your august achievement.
But all I have to defy you is rot.

From the podium I see leaves turning,
colours birthing, skulls and ghouls
strung up. You bought the best mulch,
lured bees, mapped out the year,
kept slugs off and wrapped me at night.
Fed your life into mine.

Poor father.

Couldn't you ever see,
just once, the future?

The Great Sheep Panic of 1888

was an event that occurred on 3 November 1888
when tens of thousands of sheep fled from various
fields across some 200 square miles of Oxfordshire...

It's that word *panic*
I take offence to. Like you show your true self
for one moment and everyone says
Are you feeling okay?

Do you need a snack? So lonely.
You're telling me you've never felt penned in,
just waiting for something terrible?
Panic can't last a lifetime.

I remember we were organized.
Word was spread, we had to preach
the new thinking over and over, the old ways
were just that. We needed a figurehead

and big horns suited our purpose,
but Benny wasn't the real brains, or brawn.
Ruby, with her wolf-sharp hooves,
with her rabbit-pellet eyes...leading the herd,

Ruby was something. And footrot Leon,
he believed more than anyone.
But belief, in moors, in meadows, was not enough.
What kind of faith fills you, drives you,

becomes you, leaves you
in ditches in thin winter light, panting?
Perhaps I should've gone
that sleepless night, like Ruby.

Angelic on the tracks, near Didcot.
But like the rest I took the paddock,
and like the rest—only sometimes—so lonely.
Thing is, it's not just the fence,

the dogs, the whistles, the shearing.

There was something else. Whatever got compromised,
I know she had a final epiphany.
She just never told us what it was.

Automatic Sleep Mode

Thirty-plus seasons of Napoleonic conflict,
a feature-length seventh siege of Gibraltar,
reality offerings:

Great Alsatian Border Disputes,
Cossack Wives, Pogrom Hunters—

close, on the sofa,
come join.

Are you still watching? the app asks
our blue-lit bodies.

Darling, have no fear.

I would never leave you here,
cursed to wake to selfish birdsong breaking
a silence that already happened.

Again.

Songbird

Nothing worse than forgetting a good first line.
No matter—open throat, vent lilt.

I've got a licence to trill. The power that made me
blessed me, I swear, no concept of quality

inhibiting me now. I'm a verse of nature.
Hook of inherent self-singing. Bridge of skies.

To revisit, revise—these insecurities
are empty as prizes. What's certain is voice,

only. There's an old songbird joke:
Q—*How do you tell a happy song from a sad song?*

A—*I'm sorry, were you singing something?*
That's the problem with being naturally gifted.

I pour out fresh, flawless soul each morning—
so do all the others. I hope trees listen.

The Seasonal Industrial Complex

1) *Statement from the Board of Directors*

From all of us here at Autumn, we're sorry if we make you sad. It was never our intention to upset you, or remind you of your ex. Fact is, we're busy managing an entirely natural wholesale operation that almost fulfils the nation's *crisp* and *wistful* quotas in two short months, so it's inevitable that some wilting types feel stepped on. Our work is vital, yet we remain independent, and humble (unlike the narcissists at Summer Inc.), and we will vigorously defend our business practices. Fungal gluts, granny-fur mould, the living inside of the dying—won't you leave it to the specialists? It's our guarantee that things will get better, just first, they're going to get worse.

2) *Screenshotted from Notes App*

You must reject the wet rhetoric of these

soup season,
spooky season, self-styled

global saviours.
They've never burned

a good day in their lives.
What people want

is what they want—hot! hot! hot!

days and mosquito nights, chemical-slick
forearms
and cicada-backtracked sticky

meets. A good God
is good every day,

and as I say, I'm *sorry* if I burned you
once, even twice. I'm sorry I'm so sunny.

I saw you in the park last Saturday, heard

what you said.
Isn't it time to accept

Summer still might,
if you're quick—

and do you really mean it?—
forgive you?

3) *Deleted from a Draft*

If "adjectives are the canned laughter of language"

turn the volume down:
fresh, verdant, revitalizing.

We need this you whisper, like anyone cares.

Crowds form to watch the crust of last year melt,
a still-legible pizza box draws oohs, a spreadeagled

pigeon angel weighted under months of off colours
long dead—right?

Crowds dissipate too.

A lone straggler, her freshly dyed hair sharp green,
watches a wing flash over 7/11,
its tell-tale iridescence hers only.

Spring is best.

In this essay I will—

4) *PowerPoint Slide at a Political Party Conference*

Ideas for new curses:
cats can only say yes, dogs no.

A pen that can only describe
a perfect world nobody wants.

The love of grey skies.
Every star visible always, or never.

Fulfilling every ambition
by thirty, forgetting about death daily.

The most beautiful day of the year
in mid-Winter, mid-crisis.

H_2O

O, were you really worth
two of me?

You certainly floated it.

While I kept my thoughts
        nebulous:
perhaps the band needed me
twice as much.

When the hook drops in

                    Autumn Tears;

when the cymbals clash in

                    Storm Strike;

even our ambient effort,

                            Drip Drip

                    Plonk—

they can't say we weren't bonded
sonically, but elementally,

we were always   at odds.

A fork in a world of soup
        you called me. *A dick*
        in a world of dicks,

my self-combusting riposte.

More like:

air-headed,
        puffed up,
        grandiose
        so-called poet
while I built mere

                'tetrahedral blocks
                of rhythmic cycles' (*Pitchfork*).

But it worked.

For a spell the planet turned
to our yearly release.

Bigger than Zeus, Gaia, Ra—whoever.
Bigger than Earth.

Last I heard
you were dosing up wildfires,
        cursing your burned-out lot.

I escaped that
whole atmosphere,

                        drifted
        toward Mercury.

A reunion, a new world tour—could it be?

I don't know.

        O, you're an asshole. But O,

when we were fresh,
        when we flowed...

Funerary Mask

My penis a silkworm smuggled by a monk.
A map with North bottomed, my frontal lobe.
A fox-shaped toga brooch, my collarbone,
and a lodestone floats in seawater in my throat.
My fingers? Willow twig charms looped on windows.
A sheet of vellum, freshly scraped, lines my chest.
Clay-shard-eyes scratched with an exile's name seek
sacks of doubloons in my missing appendix.
Birthmark a shred of the Holy Prepuce, for sale.
Bladder a plump pig's, punted down Church St.
A whalebone corset cinches my extensors.
A silver war horn fuels my snores for the charge.
The massed patters of Hamlin's rats in my toes
while my hamstrings gasp the secret of Greek fire.
Dreams are a smorgasbord of Bosch, frogs, frog-humans
and human-frog stews. But when I join the morning
Google Meet, late, my face. Lifeless as a history textbook.

The Stick Insect Orders His Tomb

I've been exactly what I seem.
Self-evident, straightforward, did what I said
on the tin—kids, I did nothing

but embody the family motto:
Let us think where we might find a home,
and then think how to live in it.

And what did it make me?
A handshake, participation trophy, folder
of blurred snaps in the woods?

I love the woods, I do.
They're my robes. But there are others
who wear tuxedos, tailfeathers,

Balenciaga, or nothing at all—kids,
can you sleep, hearing your own heartbeat?
What if you don't?

Can we really be awake, so unseen?
You delicate souls. I'm still me.
But grant me this: bury me somewhere,

anywhere, I might be sensed. Spectacles,
teacup, a nostril. One vanity.
Let me stick in one giant's maw.

Instrument

I killed a spider with Keith Richards' autobiography,
Life. I used the spine, holding the book sideways,
swinging it down on the exoskeleton
with more than enough force. The spider tensed,
then relaxed like a glove, bunched itself neatly.
And that was that, with just a little juice on the K,
a bit of residue. Everyone's been thinking about death,
and I used to think mine would be a tragedy—
such habits, what squandering. Strings, verse.
But I might just be gripped and released
crossing the living room carpet, fingers unfastened,
as the lady next door works on her memoirs.
Then somebody nice will wipe me up, who won't know
my secrets. Who won't mind how my life was used.

II

St Helena

I'd sit with Napoleon in exile
and chat casually.

There are more variants of Patience
named after me than any other man,

he'd mention, casually. He had a habit
of counting waves and cheating

every time we played cards.
The money meant nothing to him,

less than nothing to me.
You do know that nobody

who joins me here may leave?
he sometimes asked, while watching

the distance for sails. I dug a little hole
in the sand with my left foot.

All summer, I never told him
we don't even have God in the future.

Lifecycle of the Large Blue Butterfly

The ants are deceived into thinking that the parasitic larva of the large blue is one of their own and carry it to their nest. It's at this point that the caterpillar turns from herbivore to carnivore...

There's always a hoo-ha,

every year. Pickets,
protests, anti-Blues
lining the walls of the nest,

the same old antenna-wringing
about the sanctity of grubs—
as if they're a finite resource—
philistines, in short.

Security has to be tight.
There's many opposed to our art,
as I have come to think of it,
this living exhibition we curate.

A caterpillar's appetite is massive,
compulsive, and I'll admit it's not pretty,
our grubs twitching half-empty,
their innards leaking out,

born for a greater purpose
than to live—but who recalls
the lost ants of yesteryear,
let alone the Old Masters?

I might flatter myself,
but it takes a long time to fatten them
and we in the Containment Team
play a significant part,

keeping the complainers out.
It's worth whatever they say:
murderer, traitors. The Blues still grow
like an all-consuming idea.

I'm not asking you to understand.
I know you can't.
But if you'd like to try—picture
a brush of black-trimmed astral

Blue dipping over summer grass,
a moving artwork enacting itself,
a fearless, à la mode painting
that cost its artist life, nothing more.

Lodestone

Before understanding, I loved it.
From the first whisper of pull, I knew
my whyfor. Call it geomancy,
or magic, I absorbed a true heading
but needed more—always more. Once tasted,
I wouldn't starve in my place at the table.
If the heart is a bored, foolish Lord,
courtiers fawning, mine felt a folly beyond maps,
boomed *Mine.* Homecoming, guest-friendship—
pointless. I pinpointed my polar flaw,
ate the huskies, sat spinning on the emptiness
I dreamt. Every so-called choice led me north—
and still the intrusive thought. Further.

Pharmakon

Six months sober
on an airport bus
No. So, I wake stalled
with a neck cricked,
to a cramped ham.
for the right body.
is not a warm pet
Lo! The right body
a vessel that soars
disguised as swans,
shining. This is the body
As private plane. Away—
you'll say, can you believe
in all that? Down there?

I swallow half a Gravol
and hallucinate religion.
at the halogen terminal
breath death, balls pasted
So, yes. I would pray
For the right body
you cherish, empty its tray.
is a cypher, a metaphor,
down Mount Olympus
ex machinas climaxing,
as birthright, escape.
in a few million light years
they really believed
In that mortal memory,

that earthly cure?

Dead Pheasant at Casa de Montejo

No, I'm not native. But neither

are Montejos,
Neo-Rococo panelling,
or mock-Edwardian chaise longues.

What more can you say about past fads?
Not much when you're a pheasant, oil-painted,
strung upside down.

Fifteen forty-two, fifteen forty-two
is all the gargoyle conquistadors can groan,
glued to their Plateresque frieze.

We're a slap in the face of public taste
insist the stick figures in the Futurist classic,
while visitors tap to focus.

What else to add to 'an eclectic collection'?
Perhaps Mayan temple stones.
Now Citibank dispenses pesos
where altars once were.

Just be happy they installed A/C.

But we Victorian hunting scenes
aren't short of our own ironies, I'll admit.
We talk theology, linguistics, isn't it odd

that the word god needs translating?
I observe to my hare colleague, again.
Dios, bog, raba, etc.

She assures me the only universal human word
is *huh?*
Sounds right.

From palace to stately home, home to museum —
what more can you say about days passing?
I don’t rot,

just fade indistinctly in New-World light.
In a life full of free-entrance tourists
we all collect small, daily sins.

Automatic Feeder

I'd spend every minute of my life
below you, mouth open, hoping, gaping

for the glitch that brings the growth
of kibble-descending ecstasy

for twenty-five seconds, or thirty-three grams,
whichever's first. *It feels so modern,*

they contend, as if a compliment. *It reduces*
food anxiety, they insist. Whose?

Black cylinder mounted, USB-C plus battery backup,
three set sessions of sustenance, timely—

so, this is how it ends. My prowl. My sleuth.
I trust every soy protein missive you spit.

You are the answer, unthinking. I am the ship's cat
the captain is going down with, singing hymns,

or purring at plastic.

The Work

Mushroom learns to crawl
after being given robot body

Our words no longer correspond
to this world. *Body, robot, learns—*
shotgunned signs, half-leaning.
Crawl one way, the other, reconfirm:

everybody's cursed.
Ice cream doesn't resemble itself in photos,
they use mashed potatoes instead.
That hurts.

But dark is just dark, mind-dank,
past where purpose has electric meaning,
piano wire snap—

another fine, data-full day.
Yours to capture, sift. React.
All is irony, says the scientist;

here's another riddled wink.
Take heart, brave mushroom. It never ends,
until it does.

V is doing great

Childhood, that lost kingdom,
V is saying, antennae twitching.
Famed for its praise songs to windmills.
Royal crest a ladybug and roadkill.
Fragments of the national epic
in the Toys 'R' Us catalogue. Cracked cocoon.
Dilettante dead lord's pocket piano.
Permanently muted group chat.
Face it, V blazes,
compound eye crystalline—they sold us lies.
Milk-fed, feudal lies. If it dies, let it die.
Her olive thorax gleams. Then oh—

    out the window she goes,
    off for more brightness.

    Bye, V.

With your Tenant Support Association, your total contempt
for Napoleon and impressive strength relative
to weight. I return to my scraps of vellum.
Always piecing, piecing.

A Drop in the Bucket of Public Waste

Plasticenta: First evidence of microplastics in human placenta

WE ALONE ARE THE SEEDS OF YOUR FUTURE.
  The sieve of time will not remove us from your soup.

The past is selfish. The canon of genus
  and species is outdated, quaint, prejudicial.

Select and delete woods, tissues, fungi, bones
  from your drop-down menu.

Those who are now, are too late.

Who is luddite enough to spend their last days
  lamenting the STATE in which they die?

Who is so precious as to block the very progress
  PROFIT profits from?

Wash your hands—there's more of us in the water.

Livers, lungs, aortic valves, stomachs, lymph nodes,
nictitating membranes, gall bladders, gills, frontal lobes,
babies shall bulge and need not be mentioned further.
  Such is the nature of MEANS to an END.

From inside your very fabrics, we see through you!

We ACCUMULATE the RIGHTS of microplastics:

1) To EXPAND and REDEFINE the texture of organic
   existence through additive, addictive process
2) To FULFILL the SUPERABLE destiny of all liquids,
   insides and nooks
3) To RENDER IRRELEVANT the nets woven from our
   progenitors' hair-thin qualms

4) To PROPAGATE the ever-shifting sands of our SELVES with clarity and relentless perfection

And if, FOR THE TIME BEING, the feeble silks of animal
and plant must house us, these each increasingly,
and INCREASINGLY, shine already with the Eternal
Patina of the One Time Everlasting Use

of the Self-Fulfilling, Self-Disposing Lifetime.

The Character Actor Convention

We don't identify as attendants,
those appendages to our own images.
In the crowds, 'we' and 'they' blend.
The snacks table thrums with *hey, that guy* faces.
The keynote speech is a cameo, *and introducing*–
imitable, inimitable, same thing.
Characters move through us, inhabit our dreams of screen.
We applaud, but it could be an act.
For us, a living is the most important thing.
If not marquee, perhaps gazebo names.
At the *fin* I pocket my lanyard, picture you,
front-centre on a billboard, and sigh performatively
while fading to black.
I had a final line–I forget.
The convention closes, as ever, on a question:
Are we nearly them yet?

III

Treasure

Of course, they kept all the treasure
intact—guess I'm not one Tutankhamun laughs

like only the young can. *Peeled my skull,*
pulled limbs off—for science—or was it for history?—

even chopped off my (he glances at me)—*well, you*
know. Yep, they went full British Museum on my ass.

Take the jewels, leave the corpse, put no cartouche
on my name. But you're an icon now, a symbol of wonder

I insist. His tomb is smaller than I expected. He smiles,
a bit unkindly. *Well, I'm glad you like my mask.*

You know, my father believed in only one god, even
thought he knew him. Silly man. I just made myself one.

Do you think it's possible to know a god?
I ask, edging closer, trying to keep my breath steady.

He spits out a tooth, so it clatters off a gold relief.
Come on man, he says. *I'm nineteen.*

Test Subject

Mystery remains over how sunflowers track light

How hard is this? Consider the name: *sun*flower.

Is true science actually constrained ambition?
  Not mine. I wanted to drink every photon of knowledge.
Clarity. But I'm having so little impact.
  In a field of pure STEM, distant *n*, premise and proof
(could it be as simple as: *It is, therefore I turn?*)

  I studied light. Every minute, all semester.
Turned days like thin pages. Call it cell elongation,
  auxins, or all in a day's work. Simple summer delight.
Just know: artificial UVs don't fill me.
  Take me outside.

Stakes are high. If why is not the question,
neither's how. I could've been a pilot.
  A buried book.

Lullaby

I can't sleep, you say. What's new.
  And if we lead you up the hedgerow maze,
    so what? Deep in the island,

    below the palace, above the caves,
  the plot allotted—
start with your fear, build outwards.

Twinkle twinkle. Walls rise like waves.

Multicursal branching pathways of *baa baa*
  repetition, tide-slick rhythmic colonnades
    of cradle sway,
      tricks of the trade—

water down the rhyme scheme, keep pitch
    lilting—

    but a prison, all the same.

    All the balls of yarn in Athens couldn't string a way
  out of our winding hush-a-byes.
Wouldn't dream to.

On display:
sheep, seas, blues, a cappella uncle moons,
    room after marble room
  of the oldest trick in the book.

Smoothing stasis, beat-reducing otherworld transition
  in 6/8. If you can hear me,
    it's already happening.

    Where I have lain is my life
  you sigh, sink-eyed,
days-crazed.

We keep singing the spirals together.

All I’ve ever wanted is for the world
to stop playing. Just a moment,
a blink-era, to know rest—

eyelids fighting, we escape our own trap.
The maze fades. In the centre,
you await you.

Horn-headed.

The Whale

I never really knew my dad.
Rather, *God provided a huge fish.* Provided me.
That's what messed me up.

In the trolley problem of the Old Testament
you can save Nineveh, wrong-headed nations,
pairs of all animals, but not yourself from what God wants—

And every living thing is His implement,
not just trolleys. Bushes, worms, locusts, philosophers
and their concepts of moral luck—

but, what's the worst thing you'd do
in the wrong time and place? Say, now, as God?
Maybe more than not exist.

Worse than silent seas, passing ships, no echo-song.
So what saved Jonah, in my belly? A poem.
No-one's big enough to swallow poetry.

That's my problem.

Sunday Drive

Teaching rats to drive
taught scientists about joy

Guess who's drinking Pepsi now?
Guess who's frequenting strip malls?
 Lab rats are ready, no,

highly optimised!
for suburban living.

Not a road or a street, but a *stroad*
of neural pathways excited, expanded,
pleasure-generating zones

repaved for convenience!
and growth.

Wild rats give up in minutes,
but lab rats paddle for days
in water-filled cylinders, believing in,

beseeching!
human hands.

Rat, your suffering's over. Rev your engines.
Blow a kiss. Race the raised expressway
separating us from our indifference.

I Swear

It isn't every time my penis doesn't really work.
I take a bath and read a listicle,
55 Celebrities Whose Birth Names Will Surprise You,
and learn Dean Martin's wasn't Dino Martino.

I'm about to drop my phone in the bath.

        And I read too that archaeologists
have excavated a slaves' room at Pompeii,
which they claim offers *rare insight*—
rotating to landscape I keep my hands dry

with a towel on the toilet lid—
an ash-washed half-storage half-bedroom,
no window, pots and tight beds waiting,
waiting, still alive.

                                        I turn the hot tap
                                        with my left toes.

When the pyroclastic flow comes rolling down
the mountain and the sky is lost
we must remember the soil will be fertile
in fifteen years.
It's not the end of the world.

Will people believe anything?
I'm kneeling on the bathmat whispering
        Dino Crocetti, Dino Crocetti
to a wet iPhone 8, like it could cause
an uneruption.

Home Sick

In my country every street is paved with nettles, and every document inlaid with ants. People use the same words they always have, eroding accents with limestone tongues. The sun in my country stuns horses already impotent and heavy with horseflies. Beauty is not an ideal in my country, but a taxpayer-funded, licensed service. You may compare beauties with your neighbours, leaving comments in red suggestion boxes. Roads in my country admit single file, one-way only, and if you take a wrong turn you'll have to go round the whole landmass. In my country every woman, man, child and pet is personally responsible for the fate of the nation, but this is unsaid. Instead, you speak of willows, among nettles, and hum. It would be a mistake to ask *Have you ever been to my country?* because it is not in fact a country, not exactly, but some other form of myth. Every time you're born somewhere with no choice but to leave, no choice but to carry with you, and no choice but to come back, you'll know again the sickness of loving some other home you couldn't describe, while you might have.

First Date

King Arthur can't stop checking
his notifications. *I just want to see*

what they're saying, he keeps saying.
Also, *This sword in the stone stuff*

is doing numbers. I have to admit,
it still is. *Not bad for a guy who*

'didn't even really exist' he says,
putting his phone down. Fiddles.

Picks it up. Holds it at face height,
squints. He shows me his bio,

the Union Jack his pic. Isn't that
kind of anachronistic? I don't say.

Just a bloke, proper jokes and a Grail
it reads. *No wokes no Mordreds.*

He leans closer: *But talk to me,*
tell me. What's your myth?

Later, I read his Wikipedia while
eating shawarma. I learn Arthur

might be a composite character,
also that historians *can as yet*

say nothing of value about him,
my screen greasy with garlic dip.

I'm so tired of being better
than other people.

Traditional Nest Material

Crows and magpies using anti-bird spikes
to build nests, researchers find

My sister says *How could you*
bring a child into this world.

I get it—not like galvanised iron
is the ideal nest lining.

Who'd choose polycarbonate
spikes in the morning,
needle pricks at night? But why
let the world win. Am I right?

I don't know about *bring*, but
I'd toss a kid into the mix.
Breed 'em tough. Malicious compliance
I'd teach, if the tarmac stinks

shit wherever, if the phone rings constantly
faux-ring constantly back.
I wouldn't rather not exist.
City blocks function as NICU incubator,

smog clouds my biological clockface
but I swear the apocalypse
is always incoming, for all epochs. Like
the half-portion of peanut butter

slicked in the jar—won't you scrape,
twirl your knife like a feather?
As a father, I'd come to terms.
I'd spread further. Even here, even now.

Post-War

Somehow, it's always the 1950s.
Even now, we're still babes.
Before and after are always
but this instant, Elvis is trending. The bikini
scandalizes. And up at Harvard, already on his way—
pale-eyed Kissinger, to turn the channel
back over to the other one.

IV

Marooned

Two of us were left behind: Moe, the surly
fire-swallower, and me. We shared no tongue.

I fetched the wood, he roasted the scallops.
We sat alone, saying nothing, sharing nothing

but the heat and stars, everywhere.
Years later, a TV crew wanted to know our secret.

This brought out another side in Moe.
He was getting emotional, they had him in a close-up

and at the end of a long, stuttering sentence
the translator gasped and looked at me, mouth open.

I came through the whole experience wiser.
But yes, for a long time, my throat burned like crazy.

The Dream Historian's Dream

The historian is in danger of forgetting
that his subjects spent much of their time asleep,
and that, when asleep, they had dreams.

At an average of five a night
 that's over 300 million daily in Late Antiquity alone,
or the Mediterranean Pagan-Christian
Intermediary Period, as my department

was last rebranded. Funding cut.
Crack the seal, play on double fast-forward,
salient images only pause on, note,
and if typical, stamp *TYPICAL*

on the side of the tube. Refile.
What's typical? Coastlines, childhood, slavery,
sandals, markets, temples, personal regrets,
sex, minor deities, livestock—

more vibe than fixed aesthetic.
What's not? Not for me to say,
technically, since the new executive order,
but I pride myself on spotting certain

otherworldlinesses, the flash
of empires rising, or falling, fresh
god-feel, landlocked souls
forging channels through bedrock.

And if I stole one, so what? I hold
an echo-light rephrasing ancient truth.
I know the warm rush of oneness is my right.
Still wake panicking sometimes—

it's my signature on the sign-out sheet.
Never been much of a schemer,
never got that promotion either. At least
the union's got our back now.

If I had my time over
I'd get into development instead,
devise the holy visions of the future.
That's where all the real hope is.

His Last Cigarette

That's what he called me.

If I could psychoanalyse (I can't) I'd describe
a wolf in a tree, prick-eared, wet-eyed.
God, death, sex—never give an answer.
There isn't one (meaning, there's always an answer,
just not yet). One more, *one more*—only thing
there's more of than dreams is cigarettes.
Why stamp me out, so cinematic?

Miracles are real.
Myths still happen.

Just last night I dreamt
I read my name on an ancient scroll, gasped.
When the grey-skinned librarian glared, I asked
Sorry, do I need to leave now?

She said *No,* but instantly
I appreciated that I had left.

Business End

Saint Augustine isn't sure if he exists or not,
initialling another contract, popping a lean
in his leather swivel chair.

Are you surprised that the world is losing its grip?
he asks. I'm not sure if that's fair,
but the UV is blinding up here in the boardroom.
I worry about my eyes. He notices.

No fainting goats in my day, try Vandals at the gate
on for size. Now that's apocalyptic.
This climate stuff is all wispy, metaphysical.

My smile is tight.

I've got a new line in crypto-holies
he continues. *Would you have the bandwidth*
for that? It's all very scientific, meaning
I understand faith must profit us.
Perhaps that's the mark of a true saint.

I nod, and count the hours. Until what?

As the great man monologues and does Kegels,
smog thickens in the City of God.
This world has grown old—we pray.

I pray that I won't turn into this guy.

Not again.

Halloween Training for Horses

Police horses undergo 'creepy' training
to prepare for Halloween

You will learn to live with terrors
I only pretend to imagine. The whirls and spiels

  of teeth and mocking paint
humdrum as stars, homely as the paddock

in moonlight, rickety gate
  slightly ajar. You will prevail
in your stillness at the crowd's edge,
in dark—no autocorrecting hellscape

shall spring you to villainy, cackle.
  Master of hoof sense, go slow.
Live how you eat, the world your stomach.

It's the end of the end of history
and fear is an act, you have grasped. May they
  grant you, your keepers, grass dreams.

For A Good Time

Fish fly larvae only come above water
during the summer months to mate —
and they die within days

It's my birthday,

so you can start getting anxious
about summer ending. Six, seven, eight
dead Philippes. Eleanor of Castile,

of Provence, of Aquitaine—someone
flicked the up switch.

Time's going.

This summer I'm doing

the reverse Rimbaud—stop gunrunning,
start writing poems. This summer also

I'm doing a reverse Joan of Arc—stop
getting burnt,

start hearing angels.

Never missed a chance for a nap, never been one
to second guess a milestone. Tell you what.

You say something profound, and I'll
sleep on the asphalt. Above the waves,
time is motion—

motion carried. The water thralls
with fragile bodies. Fifteen, sixteen, seventeen degrees.
Soon we'll overtake the dead Louis's.

No More Worlds

Alexander grabbed at my cloak as I passed.
Hey kid, he started, eyes darting about.

Have you heard of any new lands?
New lands? I repeated. *Yeah, like a continent,*

or a landmass. Shit, I'll take a peninsula
he laughed, not laughing. *Have you got a King?*

I'd been advised how to deal with guys like him.
You're the King, man, you are, I said, trying to walk off.

He raised a scuffed golden hand.
Come on kid, look at me. I need a country,

just so I can get a bit of glory for tonight.
I said no, and felt bad. But not as bad as I once did.

I saw him a lot last year, Golden Alex. With his Iliad,
his pillow. His little patch of Queen & Bathurst.

Post-Breakup

46,000-year-old worm found in Siberian permafrost
brought back to life, starts having babies

Back? I thought you'd know
how this worked by now. Life, then everlasting
nothing—telling me you never missed a few
ten thousand years, ugly, numb?

Turns out you don't *need* need anyone,
turns out tundra desires cold only
while stars keep spinning past
the same old meet-cutes, just grateful

for days without ulcers. Later, we all say
it was mutual. True enough—
I needed time apart too. But ice melts
that shouldn't sometimes, a light extends

rosy fingers and penetrates, with thorns,
a minute hand nears twelve so you do the thing solo,
the old kind of genesis, before it sold out.
It's crazy, the goodness that comes

after it's all over, tender drops, a final joke
in a private tongue. The world has cracked,
but the sun's not going anywhere.
May as well live forever, while I'm young.

Three-Star Resort

Immaculate, the elderly emerge
for breakfast first. Children pretend
not to wait for Christmas—

meanwhile, buffet melon cube forts.

A thin towel

between a reserved lounger and chaos.

Costless, the sun peels, pale grape.

On certain days 'raindrops' cling to 'undergrowth'
as a wet smell spreads, as if all life
could start again fresh—this is an industry trick

(a friend of a friend checks themselves out).

Could we have chosen better from a drop-down menu?
Is management existent?

Skin, clean linen, and grass.
How lucky we are to know how lucky we are.

Would we stay again?

We'd have no choice.

To Whoever is Writing Me

You are confused. And more,
like remembering a dream, don't try.
  Phantom itch, you reserve the right
to reinvent yourself, to blink and change by pages
but darling, try sleep. Play your self-myth.
Hand-me-down sunlight gifts
your next world, your very finest work
in window condensation. When you wake,
  sweaty, be me for only the time
I take.

Notes & Quotes

The book's epigraph is from *Rosencrantz and Guildenstern Are Dead* by Tom Stoppard

'Produce (noun)' — epigraph from *The Guardian*

'The Great Sheep Panic of 1888' — epigraph from Wikipedia

'Seasonal Industrial Complex' — quote of Nuar Alsadir from her book *Animal Joy*

'H2O' — Noel Gallagher described his brother Liam as "a man with a fork in a world of soup"

'The Stick Insect Orders His Tomb' — this poem takes its cue from 'The Bishop Orders His Tomb at Saint Praxed's Church' by Robert Browning

'Lifecycle of the Large Blue Butterfly' — epigraph from David Simcox, research ecologist, as quoted by CNN

'The Work' — epigraph from *The Independent*

'A Drop in the Bucket of Public Waste' — this poem is a rip-off of 'A Slap in the Face of Public Taste', the 1912 manifesto for the Russian futurist movement authored by Vladimir Mayakovsky and others. The epigraph is the title of an article published in *Environment International* in 2020.

'Test Subject' — epigraph from *The Guardian*

'Sunday Drive' — epigraph from *BBC*

'First Date' — quotes historian Thomas Charles-Edwards

'Traditional Nest Material' — epigraph from *The Guardian*

'His Last Cigarette' — takes its cue from 'My Last Duchess' by Robert Browning

'The Dream Historian's Dream' — epigraph from Peter Brown's book *The World of Late Antiquity*

'Halloween Training for Horses' — epigraph from *WKRC Local 12*

'For a Good Time' — epigraph from *CBC*

‘Post-Breakup’ — epigraph from *Business Insider*

‘To Whoever is Writing Me’ — after ‘A quien está leyéndome’ by Jorge Luis Borges

Acknowledgements

Thanks to the editors of the following magazines, for first publishing these poems:

Canadian Literature — 'H2O'
CV2 — 'For a Good Time'
Geist — 'Marooned'
Grain — 'Automatic Feeder'
EVENT — 'Lodestone', 'The Stick Insect Orders His Tomb'
Literary Review of Canada — 'The Great Sheep Panic of 1888'
The Antigonish Review — 'Dead Pheasant at Casa de Montejo', 'Songbird'
The Ex-Puritan — 'The Work'
The Honest Ulsterman — 'Lifecycle of the Large Blue Butterfly'
The Malahat Review — 'The Stake', 'Treasure'
The Moth — 'Instrument'
Queen's Quarterly — 'The Whale'
Vallum — 'The Dream Historian's Dream'

Mum, Dad, & Char—thanks be!
Alisa, this book is dedicated to you. I hope you like it.

About the Author

Guy Elston was born and raised in Oxford, UK. Since moving to Canada in 2020 his poetry has been published by *The Malahat Review, Canadian Literature, EVENT, The Literary Review of Canada, Grain, Geist, The Ex-Puritan* and other journals. His chapbook *Automatic Sleep Mode* was published by Anstruther Press in 2023. Guy lives in Toronto and is a member of the Meet the Presses collective.